INSTANT CULTURE

INSTANT CULTURE

&

Collected Poems

&

Moses L. Howard

First print edition: August 2019

ISBN 9781939423955

Published by Jugum Press
www.jugumpress.net
505 Broadway East #237
Seattle, WA 98102

Editing and design:
Annie Pearson, Jugum Press

Content

INSTANT CULTURE

I:

SHADOW AND LIGHT

Fire in the Maples

Maple leaves blaze
On the autumn hills
Dripping hoses of night rain
Do not subdue their fire
Glowing against a mountain
Hearth, flames of red dash
Flames of gold lick the distant green
Like a dog's warm tongue
Below the fire, fragile
Flaming twisting colors like
Glass beads spin and spatter
In soft whispers
On a winter tapestry of
Lost summer garments.

Skipping Stones

At the beach there was a hint of spray
But no turbulence tugging at anchors that day
My son who'd never seen a stone skip
Tried one that sunk with a noisy dip
His second one dunked showering us with its splash
Like a novice diver hitting with a belly crash
On a later trial he sent a skipping stone
That after a skid went jumping and dancing on
His eye glanced down the beach's length
As though seeing some truth of novel strength.
He said, my first stone clunked but made a sound
The third one skipped and wouldn't go down
"Which did best?" He turned to me
"Of all those thrown, out of three?"
"I remarked of the rock that went straight down.
Remember it for its sinking sound.
The second one wetted us with a shower
Holding us for an instant we'll forget in an hour
But the third held us in a trance
By daring to skip and take a chance,"
I said as much in answering him,
"But what's your answer?" I added as a whim
He said, "None as yet satisfies me
I'll skip more stones and watch to see."

Moon and Mountain

How lovely the mountains of the moon
With lacy veils and cones of snow
Tickling clouds with glee borne tips
Icy mists cling to mountain lips

Mythical more — the two embrace
Mountain with moon all over its face
Both hang on neither wants to go
Laughing in clouds above the snow

Lightning in Africa

Quick yellow light
Gashing the blackness white
Arrowing images of naked
glistening girls' bodies shimmering,
Silver drops of water
flowing over tanned breasts
To green banana leaves.
Images of bathing preening birds,
A rippling dream of delight.
Oh, that yellow light!
Sending bright flashes
across the brain of night.

Beach Frolic

Walking by I often see
These busy lovers
Never noticing me

Their soft murmurs
Rising to intense roar
Ushering visitors
From their door

The sun beats down
They turn their face
But never stare
At just one place

On sand and rock
With rain and wind
They love each other
To day's end

Then proceed long
Through the night
With moon and stars
Or devoid of light

When children arrive
For their play
Beach and land
Are quiet that day

Sea moving up and
Down on the land
Throwing presents
With open hand

Birds fly up
With elated shout
Playful waves
Skip children

About
Chasing them
Along the beach
Children's heels
Just out of reach

The Sea's Claim

The sea sweeps onto the land
Scans up and down with arm and hand
Around each rock a stream is sent
Giving notice of the sea's intent
Keeping in view a constant aim
Land to which it will lay claim
In windy seasons it often clogs
Spots it touches with bleached logs
Having marked it backs away
Until the time it comes to stay
The sea patiently divides
His shifting visits into tides
And comes at intervals to leap
Above its banks to catch a peep
Earth and sea often embrace
Sea gently brushing land's face

St Helen 5.0

A five-point earthquake shook the Richter bar
The mountain exploded like a shooting star
The plume of ash rising a mushroom cloud
To distant ears sounded fierce and loud
Spirit Lake threw slabs of rock and ice
It seemed the mountain had erupted twice
Avalanches of debris running miles away
Heavenly gods throwing pebbles in play
Down the Toutle River went a mud flow
Blocking rivers and bending shrubs low
Firs leaves crisped by pyroclastic heat
Harry Truman vowed this fear he'd beat
Below the lake now, an awesome memory
Nothing remains not even his favorite tree
covered in ash cities moved in the dark
Only a burnt landscape before this park
Birds hanging in air caught breath before the drop
Many creatures died when St Helen blew her top
Ash rose skyward rushed off and back again
Cool air and rain helped the forest mend
Healing ash laden earth covered it green
Devastation witnessed then is now not seen.

Will You Just Go, Now?

Strike out across nowhere
Stride gently choose no path
Embrace wilderness unknown
Think not what you saw last
Senseless the wild claim you
In the hollow of its unknown
Shelter not from wind or rain
From your labor seek not gain
Go vagabond hurt and free
Arms out-flung no bended knee
Be a seeker without intent
Minding not the years spent
Owe to no one their consent
Devoid of drive or intention
Satisfy all by your invention
Roam as nature drives you
Facing what is daily found
Seeking whatever need doing
Out beyond sense or sound

The Sea Throws at Land's Feet

The sea throws at land's feet
Secret treasure when they meet
But floating out from forestry
Are forts of wood and masonry
Kneeling on concrete knee
taking a stand on boundary
Hiding close a view of sea
Making bare sea's treasury
Sea lays a carpet of sand
along the trail where it ran

Sounds from a Drain

Squeeze a musical tinkle
From melting snows above
Sing a tune that gurgles
Like imperfect sounds of love

Send it fast into a drain
Dripping by a sounding pipe
Swinging a noted jingle
Spreading its rhythmic hype

Most of what we are
Is running in a drain
We are constantly losing
Whatever we think we gain

Essences escaping sounds
A gurgle giggles or tinkle
A freshet's silver shower
Where joy and sorrow mingle

Life's in the daily music
Quick ears must capture notes
For soon the voice is muted
Sounds no longer float

I met my love in April
Her flowers on hillsides spread
She was joy to behold
But 'tis winter now she's dead

Her smile was in holly hocks
Her touch was warm in rain
Her voice was a melody
Escaping down the drain

I kissed those lips soft petals
Perfumed love's majesty
Her voice escaped in summer
Oh, how that saddens me!

Six Pac Tie Plastics

I asked my wife if our relationship needed more
transparency
The day the blue tit wore the six-pack wrapper as a tie
With one ring caught on a tree limb with him nearly
hanged.
I wondered if transparent that was me in effigy
The warbler family's nest fell from the tree lined with
         plastic Graffiti
I took a second grade class to the beach to see
         the Portuguese Man-of-War
Floating jellyfish undulating or in throes of waves
which is simulated life
Beside a split leftover birthday Mylar celebration balloon
My neighbors say the garbage can't rot nowadays,
         the dump is
Insulated with non-biodegradable that holds the layers
         for air
What kind of bag do you want the clerk asks at the grocery
A tree or converted petroleum clearing the surface
         or converting
What is beneath into unsustainable?
Make an umbrella and banish any hope of rain again
In Hawaii they dream of dolphins playing with plastic
         exercise balls
Having peak experiences with air filled insulated facsimiles
My child in the yard plays in a plastic swing
And lawn chairs all setting about are the same.
they glisten wet in real drops
If again it ever water rains

Shadow and Light

Shadows escape at dusk
Avoiding sunlit prisons
On the open lawn
Flitting dark memories
Above skeletons in coffins
Feasting on the hearts of yesterdays
They watch past love's adoration
While dancing above the graves
Telling whispered tales of freedom
Striking deaf ears of light
Total dark is freedom they shout.
Throw down the tyranny of light
Our liberty flourishes in darkness
Knowledge of day we do not seek
Black prisons of words elucidate
The mark of chains on fragile wrists
Light shudders with sadness
Holding enfolding sentence
Condemned writ of shame
With the knowledge of self
Flitting prisoners of light

II:

YOU, YOU, YOU

Capture the Moment

You are the key to what we both may become
Scratch me and your fingernail is dented
Point at me, we both are targeted
Hate me, we both are scarred
Love me, we both are blessed
Converse with me, our horizons are expanded
See me and glimpse a fragment of a star
Ask me and powerful secrets may be revealed
Teach me and we discover together
Shun me and we both are deprived
Share with me and you are ennobled
Walk with me and our journey is shorter
Lift me up, you stand taller
Hold me down you are shorter.
Sing to me and you hear music
Dance with me and capture the moment

Birungi

I still hold your entwined fingers
Lacing my heart
From our last meeting
Where you urged us not to part
The joy in your eyes
Amid the fear
The quick intake of breath
Then the glistening tear
But it's done I walked away
After a watershed of love
Your heart withered they say
A desert parched that tender life
In despair, it quit the strife.

Tuning Up

Do you feel the music first
When you dance?
Or must you ride a chosen
Note into trance
Do you rhyme all instruments
with your feet?
And listen deep with every beat
We live by rhythms slightly
Off our time
It is not often in life
That we rhyme.
We strain away to catch a certain
Beat and
It's beautiful to mark
It with our feet
Smiling down nerves
That vibrate
Is your heart often
One note late.

A Moment Unique

Throughout this world
It is only we two
Feel this moment as we do
Crossing the rails of our time
Find each the other quite divine
Though we fight hard to resist
We should relax and simply kiss
We may never love another
Unless it is mom dad or brother
In which case I'd rather miss
That all-consuming loving bliss
In the wink of nature's chance
We should dare us both to dance
Join our lips and tear emotion
Any way we have a notion
Chances like this are seldom given
Many others have often striven
No one of empathy gives to us
Sighs that raise and lowers the bust
Promises we tomorrow trust
To fulfill growing longing lust
With this time our lips so near
Take thee mine for yours dear
From them draw wanton pleasure
Give to me your greatest treasure

Joy

I have sought you near
I have sought you far
I believe you are a burning star
somewhere in the firmament
I can't tell where you were sent
all I know you are forever gone
leaving friends lost and forlorn.
Does it in you satisfy
a sadistic streak that within you lie
Are you truly innocent
Do you torture with
saucy intent
making us pay for every wanton look
in the past we ever took
But I repent and ask you not
to take away the beauty you've got
But go on, flaunt it in our face
with not a hair out of place

The Don'ts of Love

Don't love me with a 'because'
Don't say you could love me with an 'If'
Don't love me with an 'Until'
Don't say "perhaps, maybe I'll love you 'then'"
Don't say you could have loved me 'when'
Don't say you loved me 'after that'
Condition, attrition destroys possibilities
About love don't ever use 'as far as you can see'
Don't say 'I made you stop' loving me
Don't say you loved me 'for my eyes'
Don't say, "You looked at me 'that way'"
Don't say you love me 'But...'

Don't say you could love me 'still'
Or,
Don't say you could 'still' love me.
Don't ever say, "I don't love you'
Enough...Like that...That way...
Don't say you'll love me when I stop doing 'that'
Don't say I 'made you' love me.

Masked Hate

Yourself you deceive
Desires unperceived
A long way you proceed
Even to your dying day.

They declare it thus and so
You just do not know
Whether to defend or attack
deny it or how to fight back

I don't need to admit
If I know not the thing Exist.
My fellows all deride
Deletions I often decide

Are beyond my intentions
Or only a part of their inventions
I cannot for the life of me see
knowledge they fancy, I disagree

Clearly you're not insane
Accusations your life's bane
Waiting while they're saying
To answer simply delaying

You don't perceive in or near it.
Thoughts are unclear of it
The idea is where you placed it
You still reject not admit it

To Shenge, About You

I have watched you from afar
Your body moves like a movie star
Every step and move you start
Cause funny aches in my heart
My eyes take in your face
My heart beats start a race
I often stop and look around
To stop my spin or I'll fall down
Since I'm finished writing this
I am waiting for a little kiss

Valentine Jingles

To be printed on Valentine cards

In the mean tine
and in between times
you're my valentine

———

You are my rose,
Any by another
would never
smell as sweet.

———

Should I compare you
to queens in high places
none I think has
your demeanor or lovely faces.
Your hair in my face glows

———

While over the countryside
colorful flowers sway,
be my valentine
Starting from
today

Yearning

If I could stand on yonder shore
Beckon to you without a boat
Ere your eyes cease to glisten
Your ear to entreaty might listen
faith from me leap over to you
on magic feet you would slowly glide
As though entangled with the tide
In that trance hovering in lacy mist
we meet on shore in a silent kiss

Pride of Self

When in your pride of self
Refuse love, turn all others away
You are left alone
with empty arms
Not even holding a babe.

Your yesterdays of denial
Have so squeezed your heart
in that warm raging cage
Until now with advanced age
It ever grows cold with
seething anger and dying rage

A G.P.S. to Your Heart

Detection
On reflection
I need a place name
I have a love to claim
Need to know
Where you reside
You could not hide
I'd do my best
Warm loving success
With a flashing G.P.S.
To your heart
Where to end, begin
Where to start?
If I have a G.P.S.
To your heart
Always know
Where you are
With a G.P.S.
To your heart...
On reflection
Where to start?
the selection
Love's arrow
To your heart

After You Are Gone

Who is talking?
I, the speaker
And to whom am I talking?
The lost love one
Moreover, what am I saying?
I am trying to make the dead know
How it is to remain after them
Everything is such a waste
Nothing is true to taste
Time passes without haste
My mind shifts without reason
Recalling past season
I cannot tally my lost
It seems an exorbitant cost
There is nothing to compare
Fresh air is rare
Why did it happen to us?
I never knew how special
Were those days
When we just
Applauded any outlays
and bided our time

You, You, You

I have listened to you talk a blue streak
Night and day
I have heard all you wanted to do
and to say
Your talk has burned through
my inner ears
Your constant crying drove me
to tears.
But in all you said I never read
In your words one little
thing about love
How do you manage to
do it
cut sweet cane life's knife
and never
Chew it.
Do you ever consider another
Person's heart.
Don't you think someday you'll pay
before God
I'm saying now I'll let you please
yourself and go.
Because if you ever love anyone
you're too slow

III:

CHILD OF THE SUN

Mother and Me

A curtain of light
Marks a line of
shadows in the room
where mother died...
And doors are rows of bars
Between us now...
Red oaks stand in grave
sun light where arms
bronzed by eternity's heat
Shift her image around stars
A sweeping sound mutes...
Mutes my heart one beat
And hands of time
Pause in their sweep
When directions are...
Arrow straight years
Between mother
And me

The Farmer's Calf

I carried a loaded gun to my neighbor's pasture
Looking for a stump to use as a target
With the meadow as range
I'd fire just for practice
To show I had a well-placed aim.
I hefted the gun to my side
While getting through the fence
It discharged in full stride
When I stood a calf, all bloody
Lay dying
Caught in that playful skip
They do without trying
The nearby house with chimney smoking
Like my arm
Discharged the farmer my way
Hurrying to know the harm.
I knew with that bolt's slip
Flew from us all feel of friendship
I yearned to bend my step,
Slip away.
But my debt to him held sway
I stood riveted;
Held against the sky that day.

Overheated Conversation

When mother makes tea
Steam jets from her kettle spout
Bubbling a threat volcano gray
Around the stuttering top
Her kettle body menacing silver
Shining smiles in seething heat
Pausing, erupting a gentle flow
While filling our steaming cups
She encourages me to drink
When our kettle cools, she says,
It's time to talk and...think.

Our Family

Let me just say this about our family
There were mixed branches and leaves on that tree

A little bit of Papa was more than enough.
He seldom smiled and treated us rough

Mother was more patient and tried to understand
She made cakes and let us scrape the pan

Brother Johnny was older and had adult ways
He often left home and was gone for days

Rosie, an older sister, was beautiful and quite wild
She wore clothes of a very different style
She kissed women just as well as men
Stayed away at night, never came in

Robert tamed horses, married a comic wife
Fathered one son, the light of his life

Thelma was level-headed, more sedate
If boys wanted to kiss her they had to wait
She tested them and teased them with her arched
sparkling eyes, instead of looking
at them she looked at the skies

Sis always watched and waited her chance
She aimed for drama and deep romance
She waited and schemed and learned to cope
Without permission to marry she escaped to elope

Willie knew different ways to shirk
He absented himself always from work
Whenever Emma spoke it was always seriously
It was centered on Me, me, me!

Sydney was never a thinker who sounded very bright
But he insisted that everyone do just right

Moses wasn't born in a fairy ring
He was designed to study and learn every thing

My Sister Was in a Nursing Home

My sister at eighty-three
Went to an aged nursery
Coached there with sex tomes
She finally left and went home
Where she succumbed to suitors
Day and night around her door
So enthralled with one of them
She was all "yes" when she saw him
They fled now there's no one to teach
He carried her out of reach
But she writes in her amorous e-mail
She is leaving an aged sexy trail.

At Middle College

Middle College has come and gone
We saw daily what could be done
spoke our saying and sang our song
Embracing life, we took our stand
With our lives we struggled mightily
The results now is
What you see

Here we stand without regret
Our ventures are working yet
We meet to assess and support
to record the now and take note
We salute the ones already gone
vow to them we'll fight on

Deborah's Scott

I knew a man by description only
Yet he was complete to breathing
His wife's tongue traced his introduction
We met through her warm breath
His likes, his loving and teasing.
All I heard made him real
Set the alarm clock
He was not so different from me.
Though I never sat in his chair
Nor glimpsed his shoes or socks.
Is that important?
He took care of the dog
Ate dinner with his wife.
Good man with true beliefs
His illness a repeated strife
Her father strayed the same path
Afraid of confusing Fate
She said his name was Scott
Is that important?
He contested something fierce
Was subdued as we all are.
I knew him by detail only
He was for me quite real
One who, worked, traveled smiled?
Cared for the dog
Does that make sense?
Meetings are fragile and limited
I met him through breath and breathing
Her tongue mimed his subtle being
With the tinkle of a musical voice
His name and words made him
As someone whose hand I shook
Eyes I sought over pages of a book.
We might have spoken to each other
Acquainted beyond breathed knowing
Both scientists by her assertion

We had things in common.
I met him through her word song
Is that important?
He as real as anyone else I know
Though we never met up close

Christina

With kids her own army
She the officer in charge
Loading a family bus
Trusting to those at large
But the face I love
No longer shines on me
I expect what I do not get
A different table is set
I am ready for adoration
His love is dole in a ration
Found wanting now
What his heart will disallow
Fuming and raging in me
Fires burning none can see
Yet I love true and strong
Still detesting being alone

Electronic Medical Update

The doctor's coded message said my heart skips a beat
As electronic diagnostic of my last visit.
He examined me and said I'd get the results later
I received the message in my medical updater
Along with my cholesterol rating and diabetic protocol
The computer was now the choice diagnostic tool
It took away the need of wasted physician voice
Anyway, if my heart was skipping then how long
Would I lose beats before something went wrong?
The message said I should at once come in or call
If blood pressure or temperature should rise or fall
Wouldn't take long just a short consultation
Inspection of the heart's pause or defibrillation
He wanted to put on an electronic monitor to record
The nature and definite rhythm of skipped beats
He checked my diet, exercise and sleep
He advised an in-person arranged appointment
He transferred to me anxiety deep concern
A consulting nurse's eyes predicted my ruin
Took my temperature, weight and heart rate
I asked if my heart was still skipping beats.
She said do you experience tingling hands.
Do limbs often late answer your commands
I mulled the question not answering at once
she sighed impatiently pumped the gauge
no answer for my age pointed me a dunce
Skipping was as if my heart neglected duty
If I did such on my job any time answer not
Life threatening never mine I forgot
I could catch rhythm some time later

The Catholic Nun

I loved a Catholic nun once
And I think she did love me
We both loved God so there was no
Competitive hints of damming Heresy

She slept twice in my bed alone
Then she penned me an innocent note
I will not divulge here what she said
Or secrets that she lovingly wrote

There's memory of her blithesomeness
As she lay consecrating my sheets
Thinking lingering holy thoughts
With her mind slipping here to there
Eluding dark unholy naught

And since I see her loving visage
In every candlelit cathedral
And her lips lisp silent prayers
Begging me to think no Evil

If I be God's holy son what's she to me?
Is she mother sister I ask what can she truly be?
I love her in the flesh nothing spiritually
I see the place even now shining on a hill
The nuns there all dressed in white

She visited my home I was away
She slept in this my bed
And now I wonder as she lay
Which way the feet or head
And the feminine parts of glory be
Where which place were they

Why I question what is past
I can never say
But I have many regrets
That I wasn't home
That day

Awaiting a Diagnosis

After reading
Parkinson's Disease: a complete guide for patients and families.

My days are set to a kind of music
Fed by rhythmic dopamine release
Hear a synaptic transmission hum;
I'm unique in the way it dances me.
The drum's a faded substantia nigra;
Removes emotion from my flat face
You can't tell what I'm thinking as I
Dance or sit in the Park or someplace
My clock's battery is running low
My fingers are now keeping time
They move constantly marking sound
Each vibration says I am digital bound
I have stopped my social gathering
My digital phone dances when I speak
My rhythm throws friendly lives off beat;
Musical forks clatters on the dinner plate
I dance missing being in step with my date
I have contacted doctors about this dance
They say the composition is not complete
The musicologist among them shakes
Their heads in wonder, lost in the sound
They write no notes to demystify Me
Sometimes the music dies down
Other times it races to a crescendo!
With cymbals raised ready to clang!
Then it's like I am suddenly listening...
Shaking. Listening for the phone to ring.

The doctor says my hands will shake worse
My fork chatters on the plate when I eat
I am an actor whose lines await a prompter
I have stopped social gathering with friends
I use the phone to visit them now instead
My hands have become my digital clock

Each vibration says I am number bound
Each breath takes some of me away
Fed by dopamine rhythmic release
My days are set to synaptic music
Electro chemical transmission in me hum
I am unique in the way it dances me
In its substantia nigra my face is faded blank
No rhythm when a body turns stiff and flat
It's no telling what I'm thinking then
Might as well sit in the park mouth open to flies
Arms dance independently, lips can throw a kiss

Keirsey's Temperaments and Me

Time got his wrinkles trying to classify me
Compare and contrast SF an ST
SF is sensing feeling what I've got
Interpersonal sharing is my lot
On my valentine's list: things to do
Send the Teddy Bear "Crazy for You"
Feelers highly resent that lowly crack
NF errs and feels without Prozac
No, sensing feeling is not like ST,
Tied in a knot, unraveling his mind
Saying "organized facts, on time.
I need to know it laced with structure
Tell me now or my brain will rupture."
But sensing feeling is all laid back
Talking it over with friendly allies
Querying them about their living styles
Then NT comes up He knows at once
He judges each of the others as a dunce
Puts on his analytical hat. Does the math
And says, follow me guys along this path
But NF says we ate after theater.
I saluted the chef, you counted the waiters
NT knows it all right away, NF says
Feel the wind Watch me sway
ST says tell me again how does it work?
SF says tell me about your latest quirk
My Keirsey reading is mixed to say the least
I am I, N, F judging everything's increase
I for introvert mental images kept inside.
Coming out to meet others when I decide
Oh, I can adjust. Work periods in a group
But it's not the usual just "Joining the troop"
I succeed by perseverance and originality
Sometimes showing my intuitive objectivity
My opposite, Extrovert is out showing off
While I stand aside often serenely aloof

My brain scores when vied mare almost tied
They are slightly larger on the right brain side.
I see the entire picture, Global it's called
Or break it into arts and calculate it all
I am moved by the visual, love things I see
But don't discount hearing I respond auditory
My response to touch is not always facile
But whenever it's warranted I am tactile
The items used to measure old IQ
Are far too vague, Inadequately few
You are intelligent with vigor and verve
Though you don't fit the bell-shaped curve
Look at intelligence farther afield
You'll gleam elements of greater yield
Many items associated with totality
More accurately determines personality
Beethoven and Brahms excelled musically
But I am more spatial like Dale Chihuly
Dr. King was more verbal, he captured the mind
While Trump in this area was a child left behind
So I'm verbal-linguistic and intrapersonal too
So when I am alone I have plenty to do
I am not forsaken, I am not sad and bereft
There are just time I need to be by myself.
Slightly bodily kinesthetic twirling in a dance
With math logical puzzles putting people in a trance
With Charles Darwin, if I were his naturalist
I'd classify you all place you on a list
Rating you on the intelligences scale
With eight being the highest
Only Externalists would fail
By questioning the question thereby negating
The ionic silence of the aloof Universe
That gives tacit honor to our midwife and nurse.

Juxtaposition

With Parkinson's I had the shakes
Doctors blamed it on the Great Lakes
They said I could pass through Coeur de Laine
If I was sure I could stand the pain
You can die in a place called Anywhere
I know Me and my wife once lived there
I became suspicious of accretion
With all of my traveling around
people do die in almost every town
They get sick in Saginaw Michigan
Just flitting and flirting around
They migrate to the coast
Before they give up the ghost
With cancer they lose their hair
They die of something in Delaware
They are sick in most every town
With that constant traveling around
They had the blues in Birmingham
Cat scans, X-rays, MRIs all scams
After they got biopsy in Tennessee
They e-mailed me
They cried and nearly died before
somebody they were good to go
They got choked in Chicago
After being stung by a honey bee
That was minor as we'll soon see
Before he died in Delaware
He had cancer in California
Just after his long hip surgery
He had gout in Georgia near Albany
Across the state friends might decease
I considered myself lucky
The day I left Kentucky
Without some kind of bad disease
We ate in a polluted diner
Just outside of South Carolina

Doctors said we'd be dead by noon
The postcard said, Friend take care
Or soon you'll be dead in Delaware
O searched everywhere up and down
For a place with no sickness in a town
I had a friend who was sick in a coma
Go anywhere but don't stop in Oklahoma
On vacation in Brazil
She came without her pill
Before noon was taken quite ill
She hastened to and isolated apothecary
They advised her not to tarry
Take the first possible transportation
But be careful of your destination
Don't go where people just die
But take a ship or just fly
Don't stop in Chile near the inland quay
Lots are cruising for a bruising say
You say you don't care just not Delaware
Places in the States just rolling around
People die on the rink there's one outside of town

Diagnostic Methods

With his feathered instrument
The doctor touches my soul
"Nod when you feel something," he says
Now here's the pressure cuff
To heart side of arm
I need to get your BP
Then what I think is a handshake
Is a counting holding my wrist
Instruments cold. I shiver
Listening to my heart beat.
I am totally relaxed
Normal, he says

Now my wife replaces him
Devoid of recognizable instruments
Listening, touching, measuring
Smiling
I am not relaxed
My face is warm, My heart racing
body on total alert
Yet, she pronounces me
Normal

The Dark

In the middle of laughter
I see my mirrored face
And remember we
Are chained in this place
Between sun downs
Probably a large prison
If we knew the whole
One short walk and we're old
I forget as my friends do
Until teeth and hair lose their glue
Laughter
In a crowded room
Shows me the clock
reminds me it is well past noon
The happiness around me
seem to mock
my childhood fear
of the dark

Child of the Sun

I am a child of the sun
I felt my father's warm fingers
Through my mother's body before birth
Wide green banana leaves shielded me
From father's red eyes

I am a child of the sun
My body is licked black his yellow flame
My feet warmed by baked earth
I am a child of the sun
Near the flat-topped trees I feel Nature's
torch on my bare arms
I hear father's roaring furnace in waving savannah grasses

I am a child of the sun
Rolled and formed by wind and rain
baked in Nature's oven
To a gingerbread brown
Head rolled and fluffed with black icing on top
I am a child of the sun
Grown like sweet grass on the wide savannah

IV:

UNSOLDERED MIRRORS

Cupid at the Fountain

In the garden atop the fountain of bequest
Cupid bent along its rim his lips set to test
Bubbles rising in the air with winged motion
Where he dropped his loving enticing potion
His love slipped gathering fragrant odors
In her garden along fern and rose borders
Landing herself, delicate lovely amid spray
Humming birds sip love's nectar waylay
Spreading bubbles with caressing wings
Mixing love's music from which it springs
Taking care whom to love or to daze
Touching those not loved with a halting gaze
Until seeing one whom she means to love
Gazing with adoring lovingness from above
Bestowing her heart's emblem and stare
Giving him her true love forever to wear
Cupid refreshed from his bent to drink
Sprinkled sweetness over fountain that sank
Overflowing her curly locks as she lay below
Catching gifts of love in her beauty's flow
Not knowing in sleep perchance she'd awake
Seeing love desired and no mistake
Taking lover to heart never more to remove
From yearning level heart's single groove.

Ideal Lovers

Carol and Laytrice

My roommate and I are both English majors
And so one night in the apartment we were just kicking
Around the playful idea of what we wanted in
A lovers so Carol said

"I want a guy who is a tuning fork,
Who knows my Middle C and
Can make me Vibrate all over
Anywhere in our room."

I said if you are going to make love
Distractions are as deadly as a cobra
I told her first I wanted a lover like
A mongoose that can mercilessly kill
Any cobra of distraction that might
Slip into our love room

She said Ubiquity is important
Once we get into a room I want him
To be omnipotent there, I hope he is
Ubiquitous when it comes to "everything."

Now I want my lover to know Latin
And fully understand the word,
cum and it means together and
None of this premature aloneness
Stuff

Well I have been playing around on the edge.
I really want a man that is sex digital
You know he has six fingers on each hand.
And I want his fingers to be big
and to be everywhere.

Well, I want a man who is Sex Manus
He has six hands and he is not
careful or self-conscious
About that abnormality. He uses all
Of his hands all the time when he's with me.

"Well finally I want a lover like that," Carol said.
Symbolic figure, the Triskelion
He has three of everything and they
Are all moving in different directions?
And you don't know what to expect next

I want to be like that too
Only we'd both have three of everything
And we would use them unsparingly.

Just imagine three breasts.
Three penises, three vaginas, three legs
Each and anything else in threes
Three mouths a piece
And imagine us in action
Pinching, grabbing, screwing, kissing.
ing is the end word Cumm-ing
doing always doing.

I was silent and Carol said,
"Laytrice, are you still there?"
I tried not to hear her.
I wasn't listening; I was on the
cell phone Texting Alex.
I felt kind of warm All Over

Transitions

It was not yet determined
The next day
A short time later
She had not yet seen
Until that happened
It was on a sunny day in June that the flight took off
They stood in the hotel lobby before the bags were taken
        to their rooms
The following Tuesday
She didn't quite know what happened next
He arrived when he was least expected on the eve of
        the wedding
When the trial got underway
She knew her life would never be ordered again
A few days later
Just before she arrived
She arrived home as the flowers were delivered
Two dozen long stemmed roses, a bottle of champagne
I love you but I can't do this anymore
Is this all there is to life?
She had heard that before

Winning Chance

The road ahead is very clear
No one in sight far or near
In early race they lined the track
All out front and many in back

The onerous race took its toll
Few remains who started out bold
Fierce competitors littered the track
I am left now leading the pack

I am composed with Victory in sight
I could push on now I think I might
But I pause to lend my hand
To one dropped in mortal pain
share victory where both we stand

Truth and Beauty

Falsehoods made her shadow cringe
being wrong made it creak
Like a hole somewhere in the sky
where havoc would try to wreak
They said she searched for beauty
What was wanted was Truth
It led her to seek wisdom of age
But the old took from her value
But no nearer the truth was she
She changed her quest to beauty
Seeking in mountains or near sea
Truth is a shiny long-legged thing
large clear eyes and folding wings
Truth looks straight at you
just waiting to see what you'll do
Beauty demurs and looks away
recognize me now or go away
truth and beauty always combined
accepting one none declined
since truth is beauty both are one,
rejecting either, you have none
What is the essence of the two?
What is seen comes from you
Your values are there to choose
Truth is yours to win or lose

Marmo Suesus

Gate way give away Stein way and hemingway Joyce's voice
worth TS. a d

cajntopss how about bridges to cross to the wolf I initiate a
great weight to write like hey day Picasso and Cezanne and
Rembrandt Salvadore Dali and Goya go Goya and David
Sweet susie Asado paint on the lace repaint the face I know
they see the rose when I say Ida Whoever said It was what
they thought they saw Dos Passos chekhov and homer has
no home but a Anedi Pirated away inferno Marmo suese
suss A suite for when I was one and Ship me south of Suez
East and never the twin Klinger

Circular Park Museum

This War Park is a Museum
Granite bases for past lords
Generals above us brandishing swords
Mounted on sculptured horses
On hillsides near stacked cannon balls
Below wide mouthed cannons
That no longer boom and call

Gray, red, blue, flags wave
Above row on row of graves
Past the buried dead
The muddy river flowing
Moving dark clouds drifting
Near each dead man's head

The river circles the town
Statues of the dead stare
From circles around hills
In lifelike hands dull bayonets
Threaten the long ago dead
In this circular Park Museum

Circle
In the river's twirling flow
A muddy water reflection
Twinkles a mirror as they go
Battles fought on hills long ago
Death and dying blood in the sky
Tale of brutal horror meets the eye

Bright sun lifts river water
Toward an impassioned sky
Seeking, raising by-gone images
Where the silent dead soldiers lie
Fragile watery clouds rising spin
Momentary replicas of the dead men
across the gray landscape

Unsoldered Mirrors

To know who died but be devoid of personal ID
Leaves us searching for lost Identity
Today we fall in line
Accepting a different Paradigm
And the kids sing as though entranced
Greatest in the world and more advanced
I know who I was but now
Hiding my bleeding head
Giving birth to dragons
From drops where I bled
And those Fair
With whom we Sup
And shared with them
The winner's cup

Lest the world think me weak
When I am at a dominate peak
I Lash out demonstrate strength.
Yet Open wider the wound's length
We've lost the ideal of born free
Children chorused as though entranced
No country is better or more advanced
But everywhere in chains
Born free of natural guilt fears
Unless cries of guilt from peers

We are lost and left
Confused disoriented and bereft
Searching for a new Paradigm
A different mythology
That fits our time
Guernica's fragments scattered
Asunder in red cubistic streaks
Passion's eternal useless motion
Rising in endless searing peaks

Here witness a mad artist's notion
Art bringing to age creators in fire
Fostering anger's stance of devotion
A world of constant flaming ire

Nurses taunted Traumatized
By a vibrating center
Soaring wings clipped
Claimed identity actualized
My landscape wavers
A claim on former identity

Nature's camera blurred unfocused eyes
Hanging precariously in unclaimed skies
Believers chant as though entranced
Our world is the more advanced
Cloud loving twists of steel
Arches reminiscent of legions of Rome
Changes weapons and shield
Confuses direction of home

Have not the conscripted foe
Who entered yon sacred hall
Eaten the gate keepers' "lore"
Weapons shields and all
Leaving lasting anonymity
Fingers pointing back to fire
Amid fierce shouts of Enmity
And worldwide cries of ire

A fraternity of superior beings
Communicating incoherently
While lower ranks in disdain
Tortured if they dare claim
Prometheus' Fire or flame
Passed from Olympus to man
Kindling Abel's feud with Cain
Which of the brothers am I?

Kinships challenged by
Puffs of smoke and fire

From the burnished wings
Of Fabricated Angels
Smoking pipes of fate
Singed the virginal hairs
Of false ideologies
Weaving smoke

Pointed passioned fingers
Skyward to Earth
Past glories escaped
Into yesterday's volcanic breath

Glorifying the eagle that picks
The bones of sacrifice
Seared with ghostly flashes

The consciousness of those left
Lost they in the falseness
Of warped mirrors
Of Greek and Roman protocol
That vision of ourselves
Formed by mushroom cloud all
Or black glossy volcanic mirrors
Send un-silvered images
To fog-laden mirrors in our brains

Blind Boatman's crooked finger
Retrieves the independence coin
From my long-sealed eyes
Gone, but still held close
Are imagines once glorified?
Scarlet bright and azure
To the front of our orbs
Seeking identity through
A dismal broken self image

Fading with the revolutions
Of battle field worlds
Bleak choice pain existing ways
Forever vulnerable

Here is your chance to once see
Your mirror is me
Paralyzed at that moment
Drained of beauty's flow
Looking and gasping

Still in disbelief as the years go
Fore defined and brought to face
An incomprehensive reality
Sculptured by time's pace

Seared by mortality's flame,
Though we are born to doubt
Build cities of invulnerability
Nothing may touch or prove out
Veins or valves that feed
Where chest's fire bleeds
Still, in an angry sky

Seeking the escaped self

Burning stumps wave in ire
If we are what we say then who
Are they who, defined by
Our living code
Who defined us in return?
Promise we knew and now
Crave fled with those fused aerial
Breaths of yesteryear all was
But a facade perpetrated by fear
That lying mirrors project
Can't lie when they exhale fire!

Corroborate identities long mistook
Those who would destroy
What was never ours?
False mirrors that ego built
Never did exist
Outside ourselves

Never solidly in our midst
We played long unassigned roles
That built for all idols unending praise
Composing ourselves a failing rhapsody
Remade the stars, and bade them shine
As we so designed them to do

Now not we to face our true identity,
Hidden before and now we share the road
Where once all our person blocked
The passing space filling each gate
Controlling bridges leading to great vistas

With golden paddles our sheltered boats
Speed along the river Lethe,
Global coins covering our eyes
Seeing not the anguish of others
Extinguishing fires of countless desires
Machines roar out as if entranced
Made by the greatest and most advanced

Praying in the mixed language of Caesar
Received Caesar's gifts. Making gods
With treasures taken from the earth,

Bellowing in swirling flames on
skyward stairways to oblivion
Our machines repeat as if entranced
Greatest ever and far far advanced

No wonder we didn't recognize ourselves
For you made yourself in blindness

Born with a preformed vision
That no longer depended on light
And now you listen for the swishing
Oars of the blind boatman
That's our plight

Your name was your legacy
All you surveyed was yours we like who we are
And everybody wants to be like us.
We are not courteous
There's no need to be
No one expects that of masters
no one dictates we are born free
Crowds wail as if entranced
We are the great on earth and further advanced

But memory restores reality
Pandemonium, Chaos swirling,
Burning, hissing down sky stairways
Twin snakes black liquid swirls
Of fire presaging judgment day

Be brash and demanding
That's becoming who you are
We can have whatever we want
If you don't give it we can take it
We even take you as our gift to ourselves
If you are not on our side you are against us
And you will pay for it with whatever of you remains

We don't always consult our friends and
We change them as often. As we desire
We are wealthy and we don't always share
Around the world people associate us
With Zeus, the Olympian God.

Resentments are memorials at the foot of Olympus
We have the fire and even Zeus is afraid
The strongest, richest and most successful hot crew
And competitors don't like that
They exhale epithets ending in silent thoughts

Afraid to utter aloud the belief love is what we got?
Our misplaced bombs kill the innocent
And we cry for worthy innocents to protect
You cry for identity, but mirrored faces
May tell you more of who you are

Kneeling women pray as if entranced
Our people here are far and above advanced

What we have we used with God's blessing?
We are only the moral users of death
We kill to save the selected survivors
And we mourn only for our favorites
Our selected survivors

V:

KICKING IT

Ballet on the Soccer Field

Now winged like Mercury's feet
married to the wind's beat
Tapping twisting
Baubles in air where
other players have been
Body perfectly balanced
sending an arrowed pellet
With accurate aim
through an opposing net
Threading upright bars
A mystic in the game
one of its greatest stars
Every muscle sings
Inscribing circles, angles,
geometric things

Drug Scene

Sex for drugs
Drugs for sex
I got the bung
What's next
Bought chronic on the scene
had one hit made me mean
Need more to make me high
Stealing stuff on the sly

If I Die Without ID

If I die in the CD
How in the hell will mom know it's me
They find bodies without fingered hands
With tattoos on their heads and cans
Silver balls hanging from tongues and lips
Spiders and devils on their hips
Labials and foreskins ornamented navels
Look and pry as much as they are able
Where I'm at then there ain't no cable
Cell phones no longer ring.
I can't call and say I'm doing my thing.
If I die in the CD
I'm with the Homies, Mom
Don't search for me

Reunion Rap

Kan you kick this thang?
trying to find out if you kan hang
I wanna go back to my roots
Pyramids and loud hoots.
Terrel used to call me Old G
I haven't changed as far as I can see
I wanna kick it with the homies in the CD
But it's too dangerous there to even pee
Nothing like back in the day
Nobody's got your back
Your life's in play
I wrote this poem to let you know
In case you missed out,
I'm telling you so.
Peace out,
Old G

Flying

His wings for flight made of smoke
Two jets from his nose was no joke
As he exhaled he rose
Mind dancing on toes
Often in his veins
He heard blood sing
He actually flew
A time or two
No clue of elevation
But felt rising sensation
Had trouble with the landing gear
His breath stopped his sense to hear
Something beating where he could feel it
But he flew as often as he could fuel it
Whenever he took a hit
Or if somebody's pipe was lit

Frag It

Can't sit
Nit pick
dumb wit
Shit spit
quit it
Half lit
buried in it

I Want You Back

Honey I know
Your boyfriend is maxed
That's why I've been sacked
You are already packed
But baby I need you back

The sewer is open
I'm holding the cover
He is already in it
I mean your lover
Go unpack
'Cause I need you back

Baby, baby don't
don't make me bleed
'Cause I'm in need
don't give me the sack
I want you b aaa ack!

Honey please cut me some slack
I'm on the true love track
I'm no maniac
'Cause I need you back

Put back
Your clothes
Come let me rub your toes
Don't put on
your clothes
I want—I want you back

In the Rush

In the rush, when you pass it through
you get a buzz or a beep
If it is attracted you will hear a buzz or beep
Flat or not unlike beer you get a buzz or a beep
Bees are round and striped
It is flat and one stripe so buzz or beep
It or they buzz or beep in a crowd
One before or after another buzz, buzz or beep beep
In an area where they buzz or beep
It can buzz or beep on or off
It's the stripe if it's flat unlike beer
beep beep

Instant Culture

Lose your ring on the bars?

Is there need of pleasure?
Skin the cat at your leisure
You can turn inside out
It's a big risk factor
can you skin the cat
on monkey bars flip up
skin the cat and say see it!
Do it and see stars
your eyes shine on monkey bars
the ring around you long lost
monkey bar or the cat's cost?
Do you sit at dances
you see that shiny star
Cat shimmy on the monkey bar

Remember air blossomed birds
ring around the monkey bar
All chained with the ring lost
Your ring became the thing
Lost on monkey bars of night
Flip, do the monkey right
upside down
Don't lose that ring
So many ways to lose that thing?

Music and Life

Like the lives of some
Some people are born to sing only
song titles.
they never arrive at the melody
The music of their lives is cut short
When they hit a beautiful note
They can't hold it
it sinks to a lower octave
then hitting a sudden sad note
they exhale and... expire...

Sewer Sounds

Floating seeds
Essence of my invention
From the side of my house
From my house
A note top the world
Tires of a parked vehicle
Beside a school
Note on a piece of paper
An old newspaper
Some lives
From a hospital
from a bed
from a playground
From a nuclear plant water waste hot radiation
Blood and water music of its spray and mixture
On a battle field

Romantic Technology

She had a Bluetooth in her ear
An iPod in her hand
Texting on the iPhone
Or tweeting to her man

My computer is on-line
E-mail is synced
I need your web page
Please give me the link

Use any interface
Yahoo Goggle Search
Electronic engines
Or iPad I can touch

Thumb drive ready
For his mega bites
Disks like arms steady
iPhone 4 held tight

Blog or Text me
By skype or e-mail too
Holler back at me
Whatever you need to do

PowerPoint Excel
Hypertext coded Pixel
All info on your cell
Cyber world ritual

Inflated cyber space
Bubbling You-tubes Whirl
Updated Book Face
Eyes of lovely girl

On handset e-trace
Whatever gone missing
Out in My Space

Hurry! Message me
Hum to me iTunes
Don't neglect me
Send me sweet Runes

Stephanie

Sing Stephanie to you or she'll
board the Trance-Bound Train
alone she whirls into some shadowy place
and closes the door a world away
Her thin arrowed person pierces the dome of sky
Her wistful mirror smiling at a personal phantom
She heeds not your flute notes
Tunes like waves from some other ocean
Beats away the cadence of her being
She pirouettes on Fate's rostrum.
She's poised to act but listens for her exit cue
The owner has vacated the apartment of the eyes
Limbs glide in indecisive sway
Stephanie's will-of-the wisp sprite
Alight in alien time and place
Sing Stephanie away from the rail
Or she'll board the Trance-Bound Train

What Do I Know?

Through days I glide in-out of conscious dreams
Hitting life's reality at its luminous seams

Sliding, drifting this and that to know
In the river of forgetfulness my errant paddles row

My mind ablaze, grasping bits clear
While clothed in true Sanity I always appear.

Not What You See

You see me but I'm not
to be caught
I could but I wouldn't
I'm not that
I shouldn't
no I'm not.
I won't with that be caught.
can't won't be bought
you can't see me you don't
think you will but you won't
See me as me
a bush or tree greeting dogs
in your forest
lying as a log gathering
leaves of excrement.
I have a sense
of being me
separate
I desire it as they say,
Living and doing
not saying it as they say
You think I would but I won't

When I Could See and Move

When I could see and move
I put things inside of me
Inside of me changed
Things outside of me
Changed what was inside
I wanted more change
Inside was undiscovered terrain
spread out in convoluted space
folded like a blank blanket
I mixed what was outside
And again put it inside of me
It changed my vision of the
world and all that's in it
Brushing against the inside
It changed the world around
Around over the entire map
It sparked the nerves
And sizzled the private hair
I mixed the world outside
Sending it inside of me
Stars on earth visited me
The firmament upside down
Flipped a turn and twist

Kicking It

Life is a small ball
Rolling on the ground,
In front of you...
You kick it.
It goes straight or flies on a side course
Always following it, you kick it again.
Where ever that ball of life rolls you follow—
Always kicking it.
You're kicking it.
Life is sometimes a stone lying in your path.
You kick it!
It hurts your foot. It flies into the bushes. You kick it
        again and again.
You are lost in the bushes of life; but you're kicking it...
        kicking it.
It strikes a wall. Rolls...rolls into the gutter.
You follow. Always kicking it.
Life is often a hard stone rolling and we are following.
Following.
And kicking it
We are always kicking it.

VI:

A MICROCOSM: FRAGMENTS

1.
Bright Summer Sun

Bright summer sun reflecting of your radiant joyful beauty
along the Ruston Way Esplanade, the azure skies serving as
an inside musical oval bell to the flirtatious clouds, birds,
and wind and water crafts
All of this with the soft echoes of your melodious voice
heard over the cacophonic chatter of passersby brought a
subtle romantic

———

2.
The Sea Gull

The sea gull is married to the air
It seems all perfection there
Only with an adulterer's hand
It touches arm of shore or body of land
Then it stands on solitary foot
As though afraid it may take root

———

3.
Springs Hidden in Her Boudoir

Springs hidden in her boudoir
Changed into striking attire
Reappearing a stunning star
Searing us with a glowing fire

The chill of winter we replace
mind matches a racing heart
Life moves at a faster pace

———

4.
In Nature's Lottery

In nature's lottery I took a chance
Number in hand began my dance
Awards given not in my name
Numbers called I owned the same
All prizes went to a winner
Passed me by called a sinner
Winners passed up winding stair
Left me hanging by my hair
Holding winning tickets in hand
Denied entrance promised land

———

5.
No Time to Search

No time to search for the real me
just be whatever they make me
Pressure around me cry do it now
Just go on perform no matter how
Fade in and out my life's a blur
Always awaiting some disaster to occur
I lose friends by default
Emotions locked in a vault
Demands pulling me apart
'never without a broken heart'
All standards I must ape
held together by masking tape

———

6.
Long Line Low

Long line low stretched with suspense
Hung with razor blades makes no sense
One slice serves to denude a chimpanzee
The lowest line strikes above knee

Though it could deter an elephant
It's built for something more elegant
Standing harmless days in the light
A deadly sentinel through the night

Photos not snapped when women orgasm
Frown or smile thus deemed out of place
A grimace here when sliced by wire
Ignites within a glowering fire

When through the fence a curtsy or bough
Offered up the head moving a prow
Ducking up then bellow acting as waves

———

7.
I'm Wet with Ideas

I'm wet with ideas
A statue in the rain
Short people stare
If weather is fair
In wonder at what is said
They followed where he led
Dark drops dashed
Where wisdom splashed
The globe split by Schisms
Earth slices of aphorisms

———

8.
Brevity, a Brief

Sundial and Satellite
Going
Stars and planes around them
Flowing
Time Juxtaposed
With its mate space
Nature's clear aims
In the solar race

All juxtaposition
Without intention
Leads invariably
To invention

The Copyright
And Trademark

—

9.
A Miniature Copse, a Microcosm

A miniature Copse A microcosm
The world of drums and dread
A haunting chanting breeze of life
Ways of beauty and of strife
Gods of pleasure and of vice
Hiding in hollow his gun took aim
Glimpse a foe called his name

Also by Moses L. Howard

The Human Mandolin
The Ostrich Chase
The Rhino's Horns
The Sensitive Giraffe
The Sky High Road
Nzinga, African Warrior Queen
A Teacher in East Africa

Writing as Musa Nagenda

Dogs of Fear: A Story of Modern Africa
The Ostrich Egg Shell Canteen

http://jugumpress.net/moseshoward/

www.ingramcontent.com/pod-product-compliance
Lightning Source LLC
Chambersburg PA
CBHW071612040426
42452CB00008B/1322